How Do You Like Your Coffee?

How Do You Like Your Coffee?

... A Sampling of 14 Bible-Based Meditations

Series # 13

Roger Ellsworth

Unless otherwise noted, Scripture quotations are taken from the New King James Version®. Copyright © 1982 by Thomas Nelson. Used by permission. All rights reserved.

Copyright © 2018, Roger Ellsworth

All rights reserved. No part of this book may be reproduced, scanned, or distributed in any printed or electronic form without permission.

First Edition: 2018

ISBN: 978-0-9600203-3-1

20181115LS

Great Writing Publications
www.greatwriting.org
Taylors, SC

www.greatwriting.org

Purpose

My Coffee Cup Meditations are short, easy-to-read, engagingly presented devotions based on the Bible, the Word of God. Each reading takes a single idea or theme and develops it in a thought-provoking way so that you are inspired to consider the greatness of God, the relevance of the good news of the life, death, resurrection, and coming-again of Jesus, and are better equipped for life in this world and well prepared for the world to come.

www.mycoffeecupmeditations.com

https://www.facebook.com/MyCoffeeCupMeditations/

Dedication

To

Bill Brown

a good man, a good pastor, a good friend

MY COFFEE-CUP MEDITATIONS

About This Book

This book is the result of the labors Roger and Sylvia Ellsworth and the thought they have given to various passages of Scripture over the years. Find out more about them on page 78.

We hope you will enjoy these Bible-based meditations. We would love to hear from you, so please send us a note to tell us what you think—which ones you liked most, and how they made a difference in your life or in the life of a family member, friend, or work associate. To reach us online, go to
www.mycoffeecupmeditations.com/contact

Table of Contents

0 Introduction: A Coffee Sampler 18
1 Vacationing in a Cemetery 22
2 The "Thumbs-Up" Man 26
3 I Want to Hear Bert Wilson Pray Again 30
4 Reminders from Molly 34
5 Fading Lines; Unfading Hope 38
6 Skunks and Honey Buns 42
7 A Groom Flat on His Back 46
8 Sure Signs of Heavenly Hope 50
9 My Dog Knows It's Sunday 54
10 Rover and the Cows 58
11 The Last Words of Jesus 62
12 The Bible in the Toilet 66
13 From Riches to Poverty to Riches (A Reading from Sylvia) ... 70
14 The Gospel Reign of Jesus 74

   About the Authors 78
   Collect All the Books 79
   The Series 80

This Sampler's Special Offer

We think you will love the sample stories in this book. In fact, we think you will love them so much that you will want to get more of them—maybe even the whole series of twelve books.

So we are offering you the opportunity of purchasing all twelve of the stories—twelve beautifully produced books like this one, only about twice as long (each book is 144 pages), each with thirty-one Bible-based readings, all focusing on the wonderful person and work of Jesus, and written in language that ordinary people can understand and enjoy.

Check out the website for the special price for the whole set where you can save nearly 40% (over $50.00) on the whole series and get them delivered to any address of your choice in the USA!

Note: this is a special offer directly from the publishers.

Visit
www.mycoffeecupmeditations.com/crazyoffer
for full details

Collect All the Books

At a very special discount offer!

www.mycoffeecupmeditations.com/crazyoffer

The App

www.mycoffeecupmeditations.com

Be sure you get the app!

-0-

From God's Word, the Bible...

Blessed is the man
Who walks not in the counsel of the ungodly,
Nor stands in the path of sinners,
Nor sits in the seat of the scornful;
But his delight is in the law of the LORD,
And in His law he meditates day and night.
He shall be like a tree
Planted by the rivers of water,
That brings forth its fruit in its season,
Whose leaf also shall not wither;
And whatever he does shall prosper.

Psalm 1:1-3

Introduction: A Coffee Sampler

What you have here is a sampler—a coffee sampler, if you please. Let me explain.

Early mornings are very predictable for lots and lots of Christians. Roll out of bed, turn on the coffee pot, pour a cup, settle into a favorite chair and enjoy what is called "the daily devotional." This usually consists of reading a passage from the Bible and a selection from a devotional book. It concludes with prayer.

Christians who follow this pattern can go through a good bit of devotional material as the years go by. So they are always looking for new material—something to go along with their Bible and their coffee.

Hoping that I could be helpful in supplying the need for more devotional material, I gathered up some articles I had written and put them in a book—*A Dog and a Clock*. The idea was to supply brothers and sisters in Christ with enough devotions to carry them through one month. That quickly led to another book—*The Thumbs Up Man*—to carry "devotion-doers" through another month and then another.

You can guess what happened after three or four books came out. There are twelve months in the year. So why not provide enough books to cover a year? So off we went and out the books came until there were finally twelve! Since these books were designed to go with the Bible and a good cup of coffee, it seemed right to call them *My Coffee-Cup Meditations*. Thanks to my good friends Jim and Sue Holmes for that suggestion! And thanks to my wife, Sylvia, and my sons, Tim and Martyn, for contributing some chapters along the way.

One of my main concerns in writing these books was to cause the gospel of our Lord Jesus Christ to shine. It's wrong to think that the gospel is for unbelievers only. Believers need the gospel! We need to be reminded again and again of the greatness of what our Lord Jesus Christ did for us in His life, death, resurrection, and ascension. The more we ponder the gospel and the more deeply we ponder it, the more we will find our hearts flooded with gratitude, and the more willing we will be to faithfully serve Him.

Now back to this sampler business. The little book you're holding draws chapters from these twelve volumes with the hope that after reading these sample chapters you will want to read all twelve volumes in the series. These are some of my favorite chapters in the series. I hope you will read them, enjoy them, and try other books in this series.

And don't forget to pour that cup of coffee!

-1-

From God's Word, the Bible...

Behold, I tell you a mystery: We shall not all sleep, but we shall all be changed—in a moment, in the twinkling of an eye, at the last trumpet. For the trumpet will sound, and the dead will be raised incorruptible, and we shall be changed. For this corruptible must put on incorruption, and this mortal must put on immortality. So when this corruptible has put on incorruption, and this mortal has put on immortality, then shall be brought to pass the saying that is written: "Death is swallowed up in victory."

From 1 Corinthians 15:50-58

Vacationing in a Cemetery

In the fall some years ago, my wife and I did something we had dreamed about for years: we took in the beauty of the northeast. We enjoyed seeing Niagara Falls and the breathtaking foliage of New York, New Hampshire, and Vermont. We also enjoyed visiting the church in Northampton, Massachusetts, where the great theologian Jonathan Edwards served as pastor.

Oddly enough, the highlight of the trip for me was a cemetery in Arlington, Vermont, where we had journeyed to see the Norman Rockwell museum.

The cemetery was very old, with some graves dating back to the late 1700s. One of the gravestones immediately caught my attention. It marked the resting place of a Daniel Ellsworth, who died February 25, 1832, at the age of fifty. I was glad to read these words on the marker:

*Thus saith the Comforter,
Earth has no sorrows
Which Heaven cannot heal.*

Another stone marked the grave of Samuel Ellsworth, who died July 18, 1819, at the age of 65. At the bottom of this marker was this verse of Scripture: "And what I say unto you I say unto all, 'Watch'." (Mark 13:37).

As we toured the cemetery, we found that almost every gravestone had words expressing faith in Christ. The inscription I liked best was at the grave of Captain John Gray, who died at age seventy-nine in 1806:

*When Christ appears in yonder Cloud
With all His numerous Throng
This believer then shall rise & sing
And Christ shall be the song.*

Still another stone was inscribed with these words:

*Friends nor Physicians could not save
My mortal body from the grave;
Nor can the grave confine me here,
When Christ my Savior shall appear.*

As I walked away from that cemetery, the words of Hebrews 11:4 came to mind: " … he being dead still speaks."

The believers whose graves I visited are still speaking hundreds of years after they died. They must have died with the realization that their gravestones would be read by hundreds and thousands from future generations. They wanted even in death to speak plainly to the living about the brevity of life, the certainty of death, and the urgent need to prepare to meet God. They also wanted to bear witness to the only way to stand acceptably in the presence of God, namely, through faith in the saving work of the Lord Jesus Christ.

Still further, they intended in death to taunt death. Even though death had claimed them, it would not be able to hold them. They went to their graves with the unswerving confidence that the very Christ in whom they trusted would come again from heaven, call their bodies from those graves, reunite those bodies to their souls (which went to be with the Lord at the time of death—2 Cor. 5:8), and personally escort them to share in His eternal glory.

I left that cemetery with gratitude swelling up in my heart for the strong and unwavering testimony of those saints of God. I also left praying that unbelievers who visit there would realize the brevity of this life, the certainty of eternity, and the sufficiency of Jesus Christ to prepare them for eternity.

Reading taken from Book 1:

A Dog and A Clock

-2-

From God's Word, the Bible...

But I do not want you to be ignorant, brethren, concerning those who have fallen asleep, lest you sorrow as others who have no hope. For if we believe that Jesus died and rose again, even so God will bring with Him those who sleep in Jesus.

For this we say to you by the word of the Lord, that we who are alive and remain until the coming of the Lord will by no means precede those who are asleep. For the Lord Himself will descend from heaven with a shout, with the voice of an archangel, and with the trumpet of God. And the dead in Christ will rise first. Then we who are alive and remain shall be caught up together with them in the clouds to meet the Lord in the air. And thus we shall always be with the Lord. Therefore comfort one another with these words.

1 Thessalonians 4:13-18

The "Thumbs-Up" Man

It was a long time ago, but it is still firmly etched in my mind. What's that? The image of meeting Lester Auten very early each weekday morning! He would be driving to his work in his old pickup truck and I would be driving to my study. I used to tease him about that truck. It had so many holes in it that I dubbed it a "see-through" truck.

The thing I most remember about those Monday-through-Friday meetings is not the sight of his beat-up pickup. It is rather what Pete—that's what we called him—would do when he spotted me. He would smile and give me the thumbs-up sign. I never asked him about it. I never felt like I needed an explanation. I took his thumbs-up sign to mean: "Be encouraged! Everything is going to be okay!"

I know God is in control and that He makes no mistakes, but in my little, limited perspective, Pete left us much too soon. He died at age fifty-six on March 1, 1996. It was a crushing loss.

Pete was a good and godly man. He was a churchman. He loved his church and was very concerned to protect her from apathy, heresy, and division. He had little patience with those who spoke ill of her or of her pastor.

Pete had no say over the date of his birth or the date of his death. But he sure had a lot to say about that dash between the two, and he said it very well.

I'm sure Pete had his critics and detractors, but I never heard anyone speak disparagingly of him. The men of his Bible class thought so highly of him that they re-named their class after his death. What did they call it? The Thumbs-Up Class!

Ask me today about Pete Auten, and I will say "Faithful friend and a joy forever."

It was the gospel of Christ that made Pete the man he was. He loved the gospel. In his younger years, he came to see the reality and the depth of his sins and that he was not in himself prepared to stand in the presence of the holy God. He also came to see that the Lord Jesus went to the cross of Calvary to receive the wrath of God in the place of sinners. Because Jesus received it, no wrath remains for all who repent of their sins and trust in Him and the work He did on that cross. Pete could joyfully sing John Newton's words:

Amazing grace! How sweet the sound,
That saved a wretch like me!
I once was lost, but now am found,
Was blind, but now I see.

'Twas grace that taught my heart to fear,
And grace my fears relieved;
How precious did that grace appear
The hour I first believed!

It fell to me to preach at Pete's funeral. I've had to do lots of hard things in my years as a pastor, but that, I think, has to rank as the hardest of them all. In the sermon, I made mention of meeting Pete each weekday and of him smiling and giving me the thumbs-up sign. In my closing words, I expressed my firm conviction that I will, because of the glorious grace of Christ, see Pete again. I fully expect when I encounter him in the air (1 Thess. 4:17) to see him flash that familiar thumbs-up sign once again. And there everything will finally be okay. I will not be there because of anything good I have done, and he will not be there because of anything good he did. We will both be there because of the good Jesus did for us by His perfect life and atoning death.

Reading taken from Book 2:

The "Thumbs-Up" Man

-3-

From God's Word, the Bible...

Confess your trespasses to one another, and pray for one another, that you may be healed. The effective, fervent prayer of a righteous man avails much. Elijah was a man with a nature like ours, and he prayed earnestly that it would not rain; and it did not rain on the land for three years and six months. And he prayed again, and the heaven gave rain, and the earth produced its fruit.

James 5:16-18

I Want to Hear Bert Wilson Pray Again

Before I began serving as a pastor (at age sixteen), I was a member of Vanburensburg Baptist Church in Vanburensburg, Illinois. It is likely that there are more letters in the church's name than there were members of the church.

One of the members was Bert Wilson. When I first got acquainted with Bert, he was already well advanced in years. I remember him as being very warm, kind, and humble.

The thing I remember most about Bert was his praying. Our dear pastor, Ernest Flowers—himself a wonderful Christian man—would often call on Bert to lead the congregation in prayer.

Our little church did not have pews. We had what we called theater seats. But they weren't plush, cushioned seats. They had wooden backs and wooden seats, and when we got up the seats would make a rather loud clacking noise. When the pastor called on Bert to pray, those seats would clack as members across the tiny building rose, not to stand during the prayer, but rather to kneel on the hardwood floor.

Everyone knew what to expect when Bert led in prayer. It would not be brief, light, and breezy. It would last from ten to fifteen minutes, and it would be earnest, heartfelt, and moving. It taught me that there is such a thing as laying hold of God in prayer. By the way, in the four or five years that I was a member of that church, I never heard anyone complain about the time Bert took to pray. If there had been any complaints about Bert's praying, I think they would have been along the lines of it being too brief. How that man prayed! And how time seemed to stand still when he prayed! Many in the congregation would find themselves lost in wonder, love, and praise when Bert prayed, and it was not at all unusual to hear people weeping during the prayer and to see tear-stained cheeks when it was over.

Bert was short in physical stature, but he was a spiritual giant. His prayers reminded us of the sovereignty and majesty of God and of His marvelous saving love—love that sent His Son to die on the cross for a world of unlovely, unworthy, undeserving sinners.

The trend in churches in recent years has been running against Bert Wilson. He would undoubtedly be told that prayer can't take too much time and can't be quite so serious. It seems these days that we are bent on making God small and casual. We dress casually, we pray casually, we preach casually, and we hurry to get through. The God of our day is smiling, benign, and user-friendly. His primary purpose seems to be to help us cope with life's difficulties and to manage our busy schedules. After it is all over, we might allow ourselves in an infrequent moment of deep reflection to wonder why God doesn't thrill our souls. We should not expect to get a big thrill from a little God. If we insist on making God little, we will get little in return. Bert prayed to a big God.

Serious times call for serious praying. These are serious

times. Where are those who are seriously praying?

I am not Bert Wilson's equal in praying. My praying must sound in God's ears like the babbling of an infant compared to Bert's. But I do pray, and one of my prayers these days is this: Lord give us more Bert Wilsons.

I have many precious memories from my youth, but if someone were to ask me to choose one thing to relive, I think I would say: I want to hear Bert Wilson pray again.

Reading taken from Book 2:

The "Thumbs-Up" Man

-4-

From God's Word, the Bible...

Offer to God thanksgiving,
And pay your vows to the Most High.

Psalm 50:1

...bearing with one another, and forgiving one another, if anyone has a complaint against another; even as Christ forgave you, so you also must do.

Colossians 3:13

Reminders from Molly

The Bible tells us to consider the ant (Prov. 6:6) and to look at the birds (Matt. 6:26). It points us to the ox and the donkey (Isa. 1:3) and also to the deer (Ps. 42:1). So it is obvious that animals can teach us vital and valuable lessons.

My wife and I have a dog named Molly. Molly is a Morkie: half Maltese, half Yorkie.

Molly has many qualities that I admire, and a few, well, not so much.

One of Molly's admirable traits is gratitude.

Every time we eat a meal, I feed Molly a few morsels. After the meal is over, I usually sit in my easy chair. Invariably, Molly jumps on my lap and begins to lick my face and wag her tail. I'm sure it's her way of expressing gratitude to me for sharing my food with her.

I learned as a child the importance of gratitude, but I need to be reminded. Molly reminds me. I think she knows that I will continue to take care of her even if she doesn't express gratitude. But she can't help herself. Gratitude is so much a part of her nature that she has to express it. She is rich in gratitude.

We need to work hard to make sure we are grateful for God's greatest blessing—salvation through His Son, the Lord Jesus. That should daily fill our hearts and call forth our praise. But being thankful for that blessing does not fully discharge our responsibility. We are to be thankful for all of God's blessings. Paul urges us to be "…giving thanks always for all things to God the Father in the name of our Lord Jesus Christ…" (Eph. 5:20). In 1 Thessalonians 5:18, he adds: "…in everything give thanks, for this is the will of God in Christ Jesus for you."

"For" and "in" are little words with large meaning! Be thankful for all things and in all things.

Let's get back to Molly. She also reminds me that failure doesn't have to be final. A good bit of each day for Molly is sitting on our back porch watching for squirrels to come into our fenced yard. They do come often to eat the seeds that fall to the ground from our bird feeder. When a squirrel arrives, Molly immediately goes into her stalking mode. Inching forward ever so slightly, she imagines each time that she will finally catch the elusive squirrel. She never does. But that doesn't keep her from trying. She refuses to accept failure as final.

We fail in our Christian walk many times, and the devil is ever anxious to assure us that our failures are so severe that the Lord wants nothing more to do with us. But failure is not final for the Christian. Simon Peter failed miserably when he denied the Lord three times, but the Lord was not through with him. When we fail, we must not lie down in our failure but ask the Lord to forgive us and start moving forward again.

Molly also reminds me to be a quick-forgiver. Molly does

not have a doghouse, but she sometimes gets in the doghouse, if you know what I mean. Although she has to be rebuked and corrected, she doesn't hold it against my wife or me. And she doesn't hold it against us when we take her to the veterinarian. She forgets and forgives quickly.

The Bible calls all believers not to nurse resentment and bitterness but to forgive. Paul writes: "And be kind to one another, tenderhearted, forgiving one another, just as God in Christ also forgave you" (Eph. 4:32).

Most of all Molly reminds me of the importance of love and trust. She loves us unconditionally and she trusts us to do what is good and right for her. Every Christian loves the Lord, and every Christian trusts the Lord. But love and trust are always matters of degree. They do not always stay the same. They fluctuate and vacillate. Molly's love for me and trust in me seem to be unchanging. They are always at the same high level.

I need to be more like Molly.

Reading taken from Book 3:

When God Blocks Our Path

-5-

From God's Word, the Bible...

Blessed be the God and Father of our Lord Jesus Christ, who according to His abundant mercy has begotten us again to a living hope through the resurrection of Jesus Christ from the dead, to an inheritance incorruptible and undefiled and that does not fade away, reserved in heaven for you, who are kept by the power of God through faith for salvation ready to be revealed in the last time.

1 Peter 1:3-5

Fading Lines; Unfading Hope

We had to spend quite a bit of time in the barn on the little family farm that I called home during my childhood years. The cows had to be milked each morning and evening.

That barn was already old and rickety when my dad bought the farm. In wintertime the wind would whistle through the cracks in those barn walls and chill us to the bone.

My dad's remedy for the problem was to nail cardboard over those cracks. That certainly didn't make the barn cozy and warm, but it helped.

That cardboard became precious to me. Precious cardboard? It sounds ridiculous, doesn't it?

The preciousness of it had nothing to do with it knocking down the frigid blasts of the wintry wind. It rather had to do with the sketches my dad drew on it. He had been reading the Apostle John's description of the throne room of heaven in the fourth and fifth chapters of Revelation, and he was so excited about what he read that he just had to share it. So he took the pencil that he invariably carried in the bib of his overalls and drew a couple of diagrams on the cardboard.

My dad died on August 4, 1985. When I went home for his funeral, I suddenly found myself thinking about those sketches. So I walked out to the old barn, which was now even more weary and rickety. The cardboard was still there. I brushed away the cobwebs and dirt, and there were dad's sketches. The lines were now faint and faded, but I could still make them out.

As I stood there gazing at lines drawn so many years ago, a couple of things came to mind. One was how very blessed I was to have a father who believed and practiced these words: "And these words which I command you today shall be in your heart; you shall teach them diligently to your children, and shall talk of them when you sit in your house, when you walk by the way, when you lie down, and when you rise up" (Deut. 6:6-7).

We seem to have little trouble passing our political views on to our children. And we do very well in passing on to our children our allegiance to various sports and teams. But how are we doing in passing spiritual things on to our children? Christian parents should give priority to talking to their children about:

- their faith and why they hold it;
- their life and how they have made it;
- their hope and how they prize it.

And if we have been blessed with such parents, we should daily give thanks to the Lord in heaven.

I also found myself thinking that day about the hope that those faint lines represented — the hope of heaven!

The word "hope" has lost some of its weight over the

years. When we say we are hoping for something, there is an element of uncertainty. We're not sure that the thing we're hoping for is going to be the case.

When the Bible uses the word "hope," there is no uncertainty. Hope is rather being so convinced that something is true that we stand on our tiptoes and crane our necks to see it. The Christian's hope is "both sure and steadfast" (Heb. 6:19).

So the Christian doesn't wonder if heaven is a reality. He or she knows it is and looks forward to it with eager expectation.

Dad's lines had become very faint when I last saw them in 1985, and now they, and the old barn, are gone. But the hope of heaven is not faint, and it is not gone. My dad's soul is already with the Lord in heaven, and one glorious day the Lord Jesus will bring that soul with Him, will raise my dad's body from the grave, rejoin it with his soul, and he and all God's children will be forever with the Lord in "a new heaven and a new earth" (Rev. 21:1).

I'm glad my dad treasured that hope while he was on this earth, and God used him to help me treasure it as well. Do you, too, have an unfading and certain hope for heaven?

Reading taken from Book 4:

Fading Lines, Unfading Hope

-6-

From God's Word, the Bible...

Be sober, be vigilant; because your adversary the devil walks about like a roaring lion, seeking whom he may devour. Resist him, steadfast in the faith, knowing that the same sufferings are experienced by your brotherhood in the world.

1 Peter 5:8-9

Skunks and Honey Buns

It was eleven o'clock, and my wife was preparing our lunch. She looked out at the backyard and caught a glimpse of something. She couldn't be sure, but she was afraid that she had seen a skunk. All uncertainty was removed a couple of days later. As I was raising the shade on our back door, I saw a skunk ambling along.

Even though our backyard is fenced, we had skunks strolling around. We knew we had to do something. If our dog were to encounter a skunk, it would be disastrous. The stench would be almost impossible to eliminate. And if a skunk were to send his spray directly into our dog's face, she could be permanently blinded.

We had a malodorous problem that had to be dealt with — and dealt with quickly.

So we called an animal control specialist. We had read that skunks can be driven away by putting mothballs out, but the specialist nixed that idea. He told us that setting traps is the only way to deal with this problem. So he pulled a couple of traps out of his truck as I envisioned money flying out of my wallet. The traps worked. In a week's time, we caught, not one, not two, but three skunks.

The interesting thing to me in this process was the bait the specialist used to lure the skunks into the traps—honey buns! If you want to catch skunks, use honey buns. Skunks can't resist them. So said our specialist.

So their craving for those sugary treats was the end for those skunks. Done in by a honey bun—what a way to go!

Our skunk episode set me to thinking about traps and bait. Although I didn't really want to be, I was the enemy of those skunks, and the means I used to kill them was honey buns.

The Bible tells us that we all have an enemy. He is not a reluctant enemy as I was with the skunks. He is a very willing and eager enemy. We know him as Satan or the devil. He was originally one of God's angels, Lucifer by name, and perhaps the greatest of the angels. But he rebelled against God and was cast out of heaven. Now he busies himself with opposing God at every turn. He focuses his attention both on non-Christians and Christians, seeking to keep the former from coming to Christ and the latter from living for Christ.

His stock in trade is subtlety. He doesn't come to us in a blatant way, saying: "I'm the devil, and I'm going to destroy you." If Satan were to come to us in that way, we would flee. The Apostle Paul tells us that Satan uses "wiles"—devious and cunning schemes. We might say that he comes to us with honey buns.

Oftentimes, the honey bun consists of him coming to us in the form of a warm, smiling, affable, and entertaining preacher (2 Cor. 11:13-15) who never tells us that we are sinners who are headed for judgment, and our only hope for salvation lies in the Lord Jesus Christ (John 14:6; Acts 4:12). We snack on the honey bun without realizing that we're being trapped.

Sometimes, the honey bun consists of "the best and the most." In other words, he points us to the elite people of society (the best known and the best educated, and the best situated in material things) and tells us that they believe and live in such and such a way. Then he points us to the most—that is, he tells us that the majority of people believe and live in certain ways. His point is clear: if we don't want to be out of step, we must believe and live as the best and the most.

One of Satan's favorite honey buns is misrepresenting the attributes of God. He, Satan, so elevates God's love that we begin to think God isn't holy or just, that He doesn't care how we live and there are no ill results for not obeying Him.

Satan has many, many more strategies. The thing for us to remember is this: because Satan doesn't lack honey buns, we must not be lacking in discernment.

One of the things that Jesus came to do was to destroy the works of the devil (1 John 3:8). If you are a believer—if you have turned away from sin and are trusting in Christ alone—you may be assured that He will ultimately keep you from the devil's power and deliver you from all evil, but you must be sure to be vigilant!

Reading taken from Book 5:

The Day the Milk Spilled

-7-

From God's Word, the Bible...

"Let us be glad and rejoice and give Him glory, for the marriage of the Lamb has come, and His wife has made herself ready." And to her it was granted to be arrayed in fine linen, clean and bright, for the fine linen is the righteous acts of the saints.
Then he said to me, "Write: 'Blessed are those who are called to the marriage supper of the Lamb!'" And he said to me,
"These are the true sayings of God."

Revelation 19:7-9

A Groom Flat on His Back

All was ready. The decorations were in place. The crowd was pouring in. The music was playing. It looked as if it was going to be a beautiful wedding indeed. There was only one problem: the groom was lying flat on his back on the floor in my study. He was sick—really sick. It soon became obvious that he wasn't going to be able to go through the wedding ceremony.

As the minutes ticked away, we became so concerned that we decided to call for an ambulance. While we were waiting for it to arrive, I stood before the audience to tell them that the wedding was canceled because the groom was sick. A wave of laughter rolled across the gathering. They seemed to have immediately assumed that he was merely suffering from wedding-day jitters. So I hastened to add that he was so sick that we had called for an ambulance. A hush fell over the audience as they realized the seriousness of the matter.

When I stepped back into my study, the bride was

kneeling beside her groom. "We want you to marry us right now," they said. "You don't want to reschedule?" I asked. "No," was the firm reply, "marry us before the ambulance gets here."

So that's what I did. With the groom lying on his back and his bride kneeling beside him, they exchanged their vows and their rings. I pronounced them to be husband and wife, and seconds later the paramedics arrived and whisked the groom away.

I have seen my share of wedding-day disasters—dropped rings, fainting groomsmen, missed cues, and misbehaving flower girls and ring bearers—but I had never seen anything quite like this. It was my most unusual wedding.

You're wondering about the groom? He spent a day or two in the hospital suffering from acute something or another. The doctors got him on his feet, and he and his bride were off on their honeymoon.

The Bible tells us about some unusual weddings. Jacob thought he was marrying Rachel but woke up the next morning to discover he had actually married her older sister, Leah (Gen. 29:21-30). Samson married a Philistine woman who cried all of the seven days of their wedding feast. The feast ended with Samson calling her a "heifer," and she ended up marrying Samson's best man (Judg. 14:17-20). Jesus attended a wedding feast in which "they ran out of wine" (John 2:3).

The Bible also tells us about a wedding that will take place in heaven. It is the wedding of the Lord Jesus Christ and His bride, the church (Rev. 19:7-9). That's one wedding that will go off without so much as a single hitch. No one will get sick. No one will be late.

I've heard many a bride express her desire for everything to be "perfect" for her wedding. Perfect weddings seldom occur here, but everything will be perfect when Jesus weds His bride. It will be the perfect groom marrying the perfect bride in the perfect place. And the marriage, unlike those of this earth, will be perfectly harmonious and will never end.

How is it that the Lord Jesus Christ has a bride? The Bible says it's because He came to this earth for the express purpose of taking a bride for Himself. But the bride He desired for Himself was not ready for marriage. She was deeply stained by sin. In order for Him to marry her, she had to be made clean. In other words, the penalty for her sin had to be paid. Jesus went to the cross and "gave Himself" for her (Eph. 5:25).

There He stands on the hill of Golgotha. A wooden stake stands behind Him. He is about to be crucified. But He must first be nailed to the crossbeam lying on the ground. So the Roman soldiers hurl Him to the ground and drive those nails into His hands. Here we have another groom lying flat on His back. And that is how this groom happens to have a bride.

From heaven He came and sought her
To be His holy bride,
With His own blood He bought her
And for her life He died.
(Samuel J. Stone)

Reading taken from Book 6:

Where Are the Donuts?

-8-

From God's Word, the Bible...

And if Christ is not risen, your faith is futile; you are still in your sins! Then also those who have fallen asleep in Christ have perished. If in this life only we have hope in Christ, we are of all men the most pitiable.

1 Corinthians 15:17-19

Sure Signs of Heavenly Hope

The time had come for my eighth and final sermon in a conference for Brazilian pastors and their wives. Organized and promoted by Missionary Richard Denham, it was a well-attended conference with approximately 800 registrants.

The Scripture I chose for this final sermon was 1 Thessalonians 4:13-18, the passage in which the Apostle Paul gloriously wipes away the concerns of his readers about their loved ones who had died in faith in the Lord Jesus Christ.

I divided the sermon into three parts—two kinds of sorrows, four blessed events, and one crucial condition. The two kinds of sorrows Paul indicates in verse 13 are sorrowing with hope and sorrowing without hope. The four blessed events he lays out in verses 14-17 are the return of the Lord, the resurrection of dead believers, the rapture of living believers, and the meeting in the air. The one crucial condition is stated by Paul in these words: "… if we believe that Jesus died and rose again ..." (v. 14). The glorious future Paul lays out in this passage is only for those who trust in the redeeming work of the Lord Jesus Christ.

As I brought the sermon to a close, it occurred to me that it was very doubtful that I would ever see any of my hearers again in this life. So I closed with these words: "It's very likely that I will never see you again in this life, but I *will* see you again." As I made that closing statement I pointed upward with my index finger, indicating that marvelous meeting in the air.

After we sang our closing song and prayed our closing prayer, these wonderful people began coming to me one after the other to bid farewell. I couldn't speak their language — Portuguese — and they couldn't speak mine, and my interpreter was nowhere to be seen. But I soon discovered that we didn't need him as we had a common language after all. It was the language of smiles, tears, and uplifted index fingers. Yes, as they said their goodbyes to me, these Brazilian brothers and sisters in Christ would point upward. That was each one's way of saying: "I will meet you in the air."

I remember very well the loud, boisterous singing of those precious people. I recall how their love for the preaching of God's Word seemed to make them hang on every word. I haven't forgotten their warmth and friendliness. But the memory I treasure most is those uplifted fingers. Those fingers were signs of the common hope that Christians share.

How much the Scriptures make of that hope! It is our "blessed" hope (Titus 2:13). It is "sure and steadfast" (Heb. 6:19). It is our "living" hope (1 Peter 1:3). It is the hope of "eternal life" that has been promised to all believers by the God "who cannot lie" (Titus 1:2).

The hope of Christians puts a wide, yawning chasm between them and unbelievers. When unbelievers speak of hope, they are probably referring to a desire or yearning for something that may or may not come true. They hope that life will bring them health, happiness, and material success, and that they will be free from difficulties and calamities. And, of course, they hope for the same for their children and grandchildren. But such things are by no means certain. Christians most certainly share this kind of hope and the uncertainty that comes along with it. But that kind of hope is limited to this life. The great hope of Christians lies beyond this life, and it is a sure and certain hope. It is the hope of that meeting in the air and of eternal life in heaven.

Unbelievers consider that great hope to be as unsure as all other hopes. They think Christians believe it merely because they want it to be true, and that there is no foundation for it. A twentieth-century American philosopher once said of faith that it may be defined briefly as "an illogical belief in the occurrence of the improbable."[1]

Christians laugh at that definition and look to the resurrection of Jesus as the foundation for their hope. If Jesus arose, we shall arise, and if He lives, we shall live (John 14:19). On that basis, I will lift my finger and point upward.

> Reading taken from Book 7:
>
> Sure Signs of Heavenly Hope

---

[1] H.L. Mencken, https://www.goodreads.com/quotes/4690-faith-may-be-defined-briefly-as-an-illogical-belief-in

-9-

From God's Word, the Bible...

Now on the first day of the week, when the disciples came together to break bread, Paul, ready to depart the next day, spoke to them and continued his message until midnight.

Acts 20:7

My Dog Knows It's Sunday

I don't know how my dog Molly knows, but she knows. She knows when Sunday arrives. I've tried to figure out how she knows, and I keep coming up empty. But from the very time she gets up on Sunday, she seems to act differently than on other days. Early on Sunday mornings, I place my Bible on the small table by the garage door. But Molly always senses its Sunday before I do that. Before my wife and I start getting dressed for church, Molly knows its Sunday. Maybe it's the hymns. Sylvia and I always listen to hymns as we get ready for church. But Molly seems to know its Sunday before we crank up the hymns. I wonder what her clue is.

Whatever it is, Molly knows its Sunday, and she knows Sunday is different than the other days of the week. It's special. Do we know as much as Molly? Do we know that Sunday is special?

I've seen many changes among God's people over the

years. One of the biggest is their attitude toward Sunday. When I was growing up it was commonly believed that God's people should treat Sunday as a day of rest from the things that occupy us the rest of the week. It was regarded as a day for public worship and a day to minister to others.

But many no longer believe that. They believe that there are only nine commandments, not ten. They insist that the Sabbath day commandment no longer applies. They look upon it as something that pertained only to the Jews in the Old Testament era.

It's true, of course, that we no longer observe the Sabbath on Saturday, as the Jews did. The resurrection of Christ was an event of such monumental significance that it changed the day of worship from the seventh day to the first. We can see that change in the life of the early church (Acts 20:7; 1 Cor. 16:2), which apparently made it because the Lord revealed that they should do so.

But the change from the seventh day to the first day doesn't mean that we should treat the day as if it were like all the other days.

Many no longer have a Lord's Day. They have a Lord's Hour, or maybe two hours. We've reached the point where it's acceptable to go to church for an hour on Sunday morning (if it's convenient and there's nothing else we want to do), and then go back to life as usual.

Churches used to encourage people to give the whole of the Lord's Day to the Lord by having both morning and evening worship services, but that practice is largely gone. Church leaders blame church members for the loss of Sunday evening services. They tell us that they had to stop them because the people wouldn't attend. And church members blame church leaders for not giving the Sunday evening services the effort that they deserved.

Several years ago, a lady confronted me in a rather

blustery way: "Preacher, we don't have to go to church on Sunday evening. The Bible doesn't command it."

My response was this: "Why don't we want to?" Even if God hadn't commanded us to set apart one day to worship and praise Him, I should think that we would have thought of it ourselves.

What kind of Christianity is it that makes us want to do just as little as we can? What kind of Christianity is it that makes us want to minimize?

I'm happy that the Lord Jesus didn't take the minimal approach to saving us. I'm glad He didn't say to the Father: "Yes, I will go to Bethlehem, but I will not go to Calvary. I will go to earth to show them that You love them, to show them how to live and to teach them Your ways, but I will not die for them. I will not take the wrath that they deserve for their sins."

A minimal Christ doing the minimum for us would never have saved us. Why do we want to do so little for Him when He has done so much for us?

Molly doesn't know much about Sunday except that it's a special day. We who know so much more than she should go out of our way to make it, not just another day, but a special day.

Reading taken from Book 8:

My Dog Knows It's Sunday

-10-

From God's Word, the Bible...

Whatever your hand finds to do, do it with your might; for there is no work or device or knowledge or wisdom in the grave where you are going.

Ecclesiastes 9:10

Rover and the Cows

We finally decided it would be best to let Rover retire. Rover was our dog through my childhood years. When he was just a pup, Dad trained him to "get the cows." That meant Rover was supposed to find the cows in the pasture and herd them to the barn.

I used to marvel at Rover. Milking time would come, and Dad would say: "Rover, get the cows!" But Rover wouldn't immediately dash off as one might expect. He would listen until he heard the bell that Dad had put around the neck of one of the cows. Then he would dash off, find the cows, and slowly herd them home. It was obvious that he relished doing his job. It was something that made him feel proud.

Rover did a good job for a long time. But as he began to age, his interest in getting the cows began to wane. It was no longer something that he wanted to do. It may have been the accumulating aches and pains of old age that caused him to hate the job that he used to love. But the change was evident for all to see. We would tell him to get the cows, and he would look away. He might even growl. When we insisted, he would finally and reluctantly go. The most obvious change was in the way he brought the cows home. Instead of slowly herding them, he began to drive them as fast as he could. When the cows got to the barn, they would be winded and sweaty.

So there was nothing to do except let Rover retire and drop his monthly social security check in the mail. Rover seemed to enjoy his retirement, most of which he spent sleeping in the warm sunshine and perhaps nostalgically recalling the glory days when he happily went to the get the cows.

Finally, the end came for Rover. I arrived home one day from my college commute to hear my Dad say: "I've got a job for you to do. I want you to bury Rover." It was one sad job. The tears flowed as I shoveled the dirt over my true and faithful friend.

As the years slide by and the aches and pains accumulate, I understand more and more Rover's desire to retire. Having retired from the pastorate a few years ago, I can say that retirement is more than okay. If I had known I was going to enjoy it so much, I would have done it long before I did! But there are dangers associated with it. We must never allow ourselves to think that we can retire from living for the glory of the Lord. We may find it necessary to step aside from "getting the cows," that is, from those ministries that call for the physical and mental strength of youth. But that doesn't mean we stop serving the Lord altogether. We older saints can strive to excel in prayer to the Lord and encouragement to others. I have benefited much from senior saints who have given themselves to these things. I now hope I can follow their good example.

The text above tells us to do with all our might whatever our "hand finds to do." My hand doesn't find as much to do as it did several years ago, but the things it does find to do are to be done heartily as unto the Lord.

When we find our interest in the work of the Lord faltering, we need to look to the Lord for more strength and motivation. Let our motto always be "looking unto Jesus" (Heb. 12:2). Looking to Him as He died in our stead on the cross will always increase our interest in the things of God and our strength for serving Him.

I've often been asked over the years if animals will be in heaven. I never hesitate to say that they will. The salvation of human beings is only one part of God's plan of redemption. The other part is God putting this physical order back to where it was before sin entered (Rom. 8:18-22). Since animals were part of the original creation, I expect them to be present in the new creation.

I hope my good friend Rover will be there. Perhaps there will even be occasion for me to say to him: "Come on Rover. Let's go get the cows."

Reading taken from Book 9:

Rover and the Cows

-11-

From God's Word, the Bible...

He who testifies to these things says,
"Surely I am coming quickly."
Amen. Even so, come, Lord Jesus!

Revelation 22:20

The Last Words of Jesus

This is a special verse. It relates the last words spoken by Jesus in the Bible: "Surely, I am coming quickly." This is the third and final time that Jesus spoke these words. The first time is in verse 7, and the second is in verse 12. The threefold repetition was Jesus' way of emphasizing truth that His people urgently needed.

We must always keep in mind that the book of Revelation was addressed to seven churches in Asia Minor (1:11). These churches were facing trying circumstances and serious challenges. The whole book was designed to give them comfort and encouragement, but they must have found Jesus' assurance that He was coming quickly to be particularly so.

It may seem at first glance that Jesus' words weren't true. Two thousand years have come and gone since Jesus spoke those words. That certainly doesn't seem to equal a quick coming.

One way to deal with this dilemma is to say that Jesus isn't dealing with how soon He will come, but rather the way that He will come when He comes. In other words, when the time finally arrives for Him to come, it will happen very quickly. He will appear without delay and will come in such a way that people will be taken by surprise. And the change that His people will experience will occur "in the twinkling of an eye" (1 Cor. 15:52).

But look again at Jesus' words, and note the present tense. He doesn't say: "I will come." That would certainly be a true statement, but that's not what He says. He says: "Surely, I am coming quickly."

The second coming of Jesus isn't just an event that has to occur. It is a process that has to unfold. That process is laid out for us in Revelation in the form of seven seals, seven trumpets, and seven bowls. Each of these seals, trumpets, and bowls represents God working in history to move us ever closer to the coming of His Son.

The actual event in which Jesus comes has not occurred quickly, but the process that leads to His coming has been unfolding in rapid fashion since the hour that Jesus ascended to the Father in heaven. History hasn't been standing still; it has been steadily marching toward its end.

It's very easy for us to concern ourselves with the wrong thing in regard to the Lord's coming. We tend to get engrossed with the timing of it. We read the word "quickly," and we immediately get caught up in the debate as to whether that is true or false. Jesus quite clearly put the emphasis on a totally different matter—our obedience to His commandments. In verse 7, He says: "Blessed is he who keeps the words of the prophecy of this book." In verse 12, He says: "My reward is with Me, to give to every one according to his work."

When the Bible deals with the Lord's return, it doesn't

lay the stress on *when* but rather on *how*. It doesn't encourage us to ask when the Lord's coming will occur. It rather encourages us to ask ourselves how we are living. Are we tampering and trifling with His Word or giving serious and careful attention to it? Are we mindful of the fact that obedience will bring rich rewards from our Lord, and disobedience will cause the loss of those rewards?

To put it another way, the truth of the Lord's coming ought to make us think seriously and carefully about these words from the Apostle Peter: ". . .what manner of persons ought you to be in holy conduct and godliness. . ." (2 Peter 3:11).

The last recorded words of Jesus—how encouraging they are! The Lord Jesus is even now in the process of coming. World events are not meaningless. The Lord is working in and through them to prepare the stage for His appearance. Our response to these things should be to say: "Are You, Lord, in the process of coming? Continue the process until it is finally complete, and we finally see Your dear face in glory." In other words, our response should be to join John in saying: "Amen. Even so, come Lord Jesus!"

Reading taken from Book 10:

Apples of Gold in Silver Settings

-12-

From God's Word, the Bible...

Forever, O LORD,
Your word is settled in heaven.

Psalm 119:89

The Bible in the Toilet

I had placed my Bible on a table in the church foyer a few minutes before our evening worship service was to begin. But when I went back, it was gone. I asked a couple of the church members if they knew what happened to my Bible. It was then that I learned that two young men had come into the church. It soon became clear that they weren't there to worship but rather to ridicule and threaten. They were invited to stay for the service, but they refused to do so, and parted with a few comments about how stupid all of us were to believe and practice what they referred to as "this stuff."

They were gone and my Bible was gone. Had they taken it with them? Several people fanned out across the building to look for the missing Bible. One of the men soon returned to say he had found it. It was stuffed in the toilet in the men's room.

Having attended a secular university, I was used to being around Christian-haters, but I was still a little surprised at what these young ruffians had done with my Bible. That was a long time ago. Hatred of Christianity has grown so much the last several years that I wouldn't be surprised at all if the same thing were to happen to me today.

The prophet Jeremiah had an experience similar to mine. We read about it in Jeremiah 36. The Lord commanded Jeremiah to write on a scroll the words that He, the Lord, had given Jeremiah to speak (v. 1).

We have in this command a small picture of how the whole Bible came to exist. God prompted men to write what He wanted written (2 Tim. 3:16; 2 Peter 1:21).

When the scroll was completed, it was read at the temple "in the hearing of all the people" (v. 10). It was then read to the princes of the kingdom. These men were filled with fear as they listened to this reading because Jeremiah's scroll contained the message of God's judgment (vv. 11-19).

These princes decided that the scroll should be read to King Jehoiakim, who was sitting "in the winter house in the ninth month, with a fire burning on the hearth before him" (v. 22).

Jehoiakim's response to this is shocking: he listened to part of the reading and then "cut it with the scribe's knife and cast it into the fire that was on the hearth" (v. 23).

The princes who had wanted the scroll read to the king were astonished at the attitude of the king and his attendants. The king had burned the scroll, which was presented to him as God's Word, but the king and his attendants "were not afraid, nor did they tear their garments" (v. 24).

The king even went so far as to command that Jeremiah and his secretary, Baruch, be arrested (v. 26). Such was his disdain for the Word of God and the men of God!

Jeremiah's Bible in the fire and mine in the toilet—sad ends for those copies of God's Word! But while men can destroy copies of God's Word, they can never destroy God's

Word. The truth of this is brought out in powerful fashion by the remaining verses of Jeremiah 36. After the king burned the first scroll, the Lord said to Jeremiah: "Take yet another scroll, and write on it all the former words that were in the first scroll which Jehoiakim the king of Judah has burned" (v. 28).

Would Jeremiah be able to remember all that was in the burned scroll? Perhaps not, but the Lord has no trouble with His memory! So, the second scroll perfectly repeated the words of the first and also included "many similar words" (v. 32).

Jehoiakim paid a fearful price for casting God's Word into the fire. It caused him to experience the fire of God's judgment (v. 30). He comes to us from the Scripture he hated so much to tell us that we can't finally destroy God's Word, but it can destroy us.

What about the young men who destroyed my Bible? I don't know what became of them. They may now be out in eternity. I can only hope that they came to see the folly of their contempt for God's Word and began to treasure it.

And what about the Bible? I have a copy right here beside me.

Reading taken from Book 11:

Old Houses, New Houses

-13-

From God's Word, the Bible...

For you know the grace of our Lord Jesus Christ, that though He was rich, yet for your sakes He became poor, that you through His poverty might become rich.

2 Corinthians 8:9

From Riches to Poverty to Riches

A Reading from Sylvia

In the mid to late 1940s, my mother and I were living with my widowed grandmother. My mother was also a widow, my father having been killed in World War II before I was born. Mother was a career woman with a good job that she enjoyed. She wore nice clothes and shoes. My grandmother's house was nicer than most homes in our small community. Mother had paid to have a bathroom installed, which was a luxury few homes in our community had. Grandma took care of me while Mother was at work. So life was good, comfortable, and quite easygoing for Mother.

And then she met Gene Miller, a poor, struggling farmer. After a brief courtship they were married, and Mother's life drastically changed. She quit her job, and we moved to a farm seventeen miles from town. My new dad didn't own the farm; he just rented the land and the small four-room house that came with it.

The house had no electricity, no running water, and, of course, no bathroom. It was located two miles from the highway, and before the road reached our house it changed from a gravel road to a dirt road. That meant when it rained, the dirt road became a mud road and sometimes so impassable that we had to leave our car at the end of the gravel road and walk through the mud the last quarter of a mile to our house.

Why did my mother give up the easy life she had in exchange for a difficult life as the wife of a poor farmer? It was love. She loved Dad enough to become poor with him.

The Lord Jesus Christ did a similar thing for us, but on a much greater scale. He left the beauty, glory, and riches of heaven to come to this earth in our humanity. His life of perfect obedience to the Father was marked by poverty and difficulty (Matt. 8:20). Then He died on the cross a death like no one else has ever died, taking upon Himself our sins and receiving the full fury of God's wrath against those sins.

And why did He do it? It was love. He loved us enough to lay aside the riches He enjoyed in heaven and become poor, so that we who were poor in our sins and hopelessness could become rich. No, this isn't referring to monetary riches, but to the greater riches that are ours as believers in Christ: forgiveness of sins, right standing with God, and an eternal home in heaven.

What was the result of Christ's willingness to come to this earth to carry out the plan of redemption? A multitude of people who were poor in their sins and living under the judgment of God have become rich.

And what were the results of my mother's willingness to marry Gene Miller? After a few months we got electricity in that little house and a pump at the kitchen sink to bring in cold water. Four years later, Mom and Dad were able to purchase a farm of their own closer to town. It had a large farmhouse that Dad turned into a comfortable home where Mom lived until her death. As a result of the choice Mom made, she and I both became rich. No, not monetarily, but in much better ways. Mother acquired a husband who loved her devotedly the rest of her life. I acquired a wonderful Christian father who couldn't have loved me more if I had been his own flesh and blood. God blessed their marriage with four sons who adored their mom, and my life was enriched by growing up with siblings.

I am so thankful that Mother chose to lay aside her comfortable life and financial stability to become poor for a season so that she and I could become rich in many ways. And oh, how much more thankful I am that the Lord Jesus Christ chose to lay aside His riches and become poor for a season to enrich me with His glorious salvation.

Reading taken from Book 11:

Old Houses, New Houses

-14-

From God's Word, the Bible...

The LORD said to my Lord,
"Sit at My right hand,
Till I make Your enemies Your footstool."
The LORD shall send the rod of Your strength out of Zion.
Rule in the midst of Your enemies!

Psalm 110:1-2

The Gospel Reign of Jesus

No list of Old Testament prophecies of Christ is complete without Psalm 110, which is quoted more than any other in the New Testament.

I wonder what David was thinking as he wrote the words of verses 1 through 4. He had to know that they weren't just his words. He had to realize that he was being prompted to write words that were being given to him by God's Spirit. And what words! In these verses, David actually reports the words spoken by the Lord to the Lord!

Who are these Lords (v. 1)? The first is God the Father; the second is God the Son.

In the writing of this psalm, God's Spirit carried David all the way from the humiliation of Christ to His exaltation, that is, all the way from Jesus coming to this earth as a man to Him returning to heaven. The Spirit carries David from Jesus' descending to His ascending. Quite a tour!

What did David hear the Father saying to the Son? We

can capture it in the words "Sit" (v. 1), "Rule" (v. 2) and "You are" (v. 4). The Father saying "Sit" to the Son would mean that redemption's work was now done. The agonies of the cross would be in the past. The grave would be defeated. With it all accomplished and over, the Father offers the Son the position of highest honor in heaven—the seat at His, the Father's, right hand.

The Father, fully satisfied with the redeeming work of His Son, has determined that He should have preeminence in all things (Col. 1:18).

If we want to be pleasing to God, we must seek to give Jesus the preeminence in our thinking, speaking, and doing. And we must give Him preeminence in our public worship. How sad it is that this needs to be said about worship, but our days make the saying of it essential.

With the word "Rule," the Father would be telling His Son to begin His gospel reign. We must not think that Jesus' rule is something that will occur at the end of time. Jesus is ruling now.

One of the things we need to note about this gospel reign is that it will finally result in the complete subjection of all the Messiah's enemies (v. 1). Every knee will finally bow before him and every tongue will finally confess that he is Lord (Phil. 2:9-11).

A second thing for us to note is that Jesus' reign is conquering enemies even now. As the church preaches the gospel, the Lord Jesus Christ extends his "rod" or scepter "out of Zion" (v. 2).

Here's another thing: Jesus' gospel reign is manifested by the people of God themselves. We don't have to be in the courts of heaven to see Jesus reigning. We see that reign every time a sinner is conquered by the gospel of Christ. How are sinners so conquered? By the Lord making them willing to receive the gospel! Thus the Father says to the Messiah:

> *Your people shall be volunteers*
> *In the day of Your power.* . . . (v. 3)

When the gospel exerts its conquering power, those who receive it begin to display "the beauties of holiness" (v. 3). Every sign of holiness among God's people is evidence that the gospel reign is in effect. That's no small thing because those saved in the gospel age will be as numerous as the drops of dew that come "from the womb of the morning" (v. 3).

With the words "You are," the Father accentuates the priestly work of King Jesus. The king is also a priest!

This dual role, as noted earlier in these readings, was pictured by Melchizedek, who was both a king and a priest in Abraham's day (Gen 14:18-20). While he was associated with both righteousness and peace, Melchizedek couldn't perfectly represent those things. But Jesus does.

The way by which he produced peace between guilty sinners and the holy God was through righteousness. He Himself lived a perfectly righteous life, providing the righteousness that we do not have, righteousness that is credited to us when we believe. Furthermore, Jesus' death also had to do with righteousness. He died to receive the righteous sentence of the holy God against our sins. In other words, He received on the cross what God's righteousness demanded, namely, the wrath of God.

David was certainly blessed to write these words, and we are certainly blessed to read them. And we are even more blessed if we find that we are truly subjects of the King, rescued from the power and dominion of sin, forever to love, serve, and obey Him. Is He your Lord and King?

Reading taken from Book 11:

Old Houses, New Houses

About the Authors

Roger and Sylvia Ellsworth have similar backgrounds, being born to Christian parents, growing up on farms in southern Illinois, attending rural churches in their childhood years, and coming to know the Lord at an early age.

They first met in March of 1967 when they were serving on a revival team, which had Roger preaching and Sylvia playing the piano. They became engaged in the fall of 1968 and were married in June of 1969.

They have two sons, Tim and Martyn, and five grandchildren.

Now retired, Roger served for many years as a pastor of Baptist churches in Illinois, Kansas, Missouri, and Tennessee. Sylvia has devoted her years to homemaking and serving in various capacities in churches.

Their love for the gospel of Christ and the desire to encourage others to love it as well has led them to write *My Coffee Cup Meditations*. Roger's sermons are available to listen for free on SermonAudio.com.

Collect All the Books!

Visit
www.mycoffeecupmeditations.com/crazyoffer
for full details

The Series

Enjoy collecting the My Coffee Cup Meditations Series.

A Dog and A Clock 978-0-9988812-9-4 (Series#1)
The "Thumbs-Up" Man 978-0-9988812-5-6 (Series#2)
When God Blocks Our Path 978-0-9988812-4-9 (Series#3)
Fading Lines, Unfading Hope 978-0-9996559-1-7 (Series#4)
The Day the Milk Spilled 978-0-9965168-6-0 (Series#5)
"Where Are the Donuts?" 978-0-9965168-7-7 (Series#6)
Sure Signs of Heavenly Hope 978-0-9988812-1-8 (Series#7)
My Dog Knows It's Sunday 978-0-9996559-6-2 (Series#8)
Rover and the Cows 978-0-9996559-7-9 (Series#9)
Apples of Gold in Silver Settings 978-0-9600203-0-0 (Series#10)
Old Houses, New Houses 978-0-9600203-1-7 (Series#11)
Golden Key and Silver Chain 978-0-9600203-2-4 (Series#12)

Get the set for a special price:

www.mycoffeecupmeditations.com/crazyoffer

www.ingramcontent.com/pod-product-compliance
Lightning Source LLC
Chambersburg PA
CBHW050605300426
44112CB00013B/2084